Guiding Stars

A Father's Lessons for Living a Life of Integrity and Wisdom

By: Ed Merid

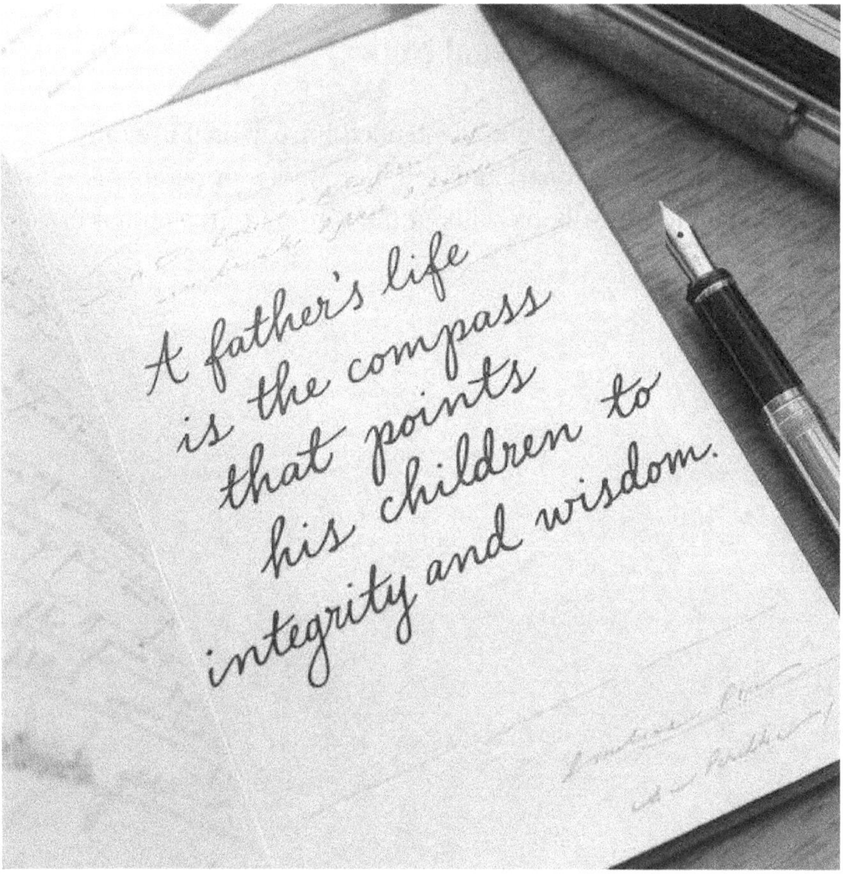

A father's life is the compass that points his children to integrity and wisdom.

© Copyright 2024 Ed Merid - All Rights Reserved.

Copyright and Disclaimer

The contents of this book may not be reproduced, duplicated, or transmitted without the written permission of the author. Under no circumstances shall the publisher, or the author, be held legally liable for any monetary or non-monetary damages or losses resulting from the information contained in this book, whether directly or indirectly.

Legal Notice:

This book is copyrighted and is intended for personal use only. You may not modify, distribute, sell, use, quote, or paraphrase any part or content of this book without the consent of the author or publisher.

Table of Contents

Introduction: Letter from the Heart

My dear son,

Today, I take this moment to write to you, not as the father you see each day, but as a companion on the journey of life. These pages hold thoughts and lessons I would have loved to know earlier, insights shaped by my experiences, my mistakes, and my growth. I hope they might serve as a guiding star, offering you direction when you are finding your own path.

Above all, please know that my pride and love for you are boundless. Watching you grow into a unique, strong individual fills me with joy, and my deepest wish is to help you build a life that is fulfilling and true to who you are. Perhaps you'll read these words in years to come, or maybe tomorrow, during a time of doubt or simply when you feel ready. These lessons aren't meant to tell you how to live but to offer you tools to meet the challenges and wonders of life with grace.

Life, my son, is a path filled with both trials and unexpected joys, a series of mysteries best faced with patience, courage, and wisdom. It will ask you to face others, but most of all, to confront yourself. That is why I want to remind you that integrity is a compass that will guide you, even through the darkest storms. Always stay true to who you are and to the values that define you. This is how you will build a life and relationships you can look upon with pride.

I encourage you to live each day with purpose, to never take for granted what you have, and to seek authenticity in everything you do. Wisdom comes from paying attention to the little things and learning from each experience, however humble. It is easy to get lost in the noise of the world, but always find a moment to listen to what your heart has to say.

These pages are for you, my son. May these words bring comfort and strength when you need them. And remember, I will always be here, by your side on this journey, proud and trusting in the man you are becoming.

With all my love,

Your father

Part 1: Knowing Yourself

My son,

Before you step out into the world, you must take a journey within. Knowing yourself is perhaps the hardest, yet most essential, path you'll ever walk. Life will constantly pull you in different directions, full of people and pressures urging you to fit into molds that weren't made for you. If you don't take the time to understand who you are, what you value, and what brings you meaning, you'll risk becoming a stranger in your own life.

So start by asking yourself: What do I believe? What truly matters to me? These questions may seem simple, but the answers won't always come easily. Be patient, because self-discovery isn't something you complete in a single moment; it's a lifelong journey, one that will evolve as you do.

As you grow, you'll change, your values will sharpen, and you'll uncover layers within yourself that you never knew were there. Embrace that change. Knowing yourself isn't about finding a single, unchanging truth. It's about staying curious, being honest with yourself, and choosing to grow from each experience.

Remember, my son, this world is full of voices. Let yours be the one that guides you.

Chapter 1: Building the Foundation of Identity

My son, when I was your age, I remember a particular day that shaped how I began to understand myself. It was a summer afternoon, and I was helping your grandfather repair an old wooden fence around our garden. I was clumsy with the tools, fumbling to align the planks, and I could see your grandfather watching me with his usual quiet patience. Finally, he handed me the hammer and said, 'Son, before you fix this fence, you need to know why it's worth repairing in the first place.'

At first, I didn't understand what he meant. It was just a fence to me; a simple barrier around a patch of flowers and vegetables. But he explained that the fence wasn't just wood and nails; it represented effort, care, and protection for the things we valued inside. 'When you build or repair something,' he said, 'you're defining its purpose and worth. The same goes for yourself. Before you can grow, you need to know what you stand for and why.'

That day stayed with me because it was about more than the fence. I began to think about what I valued and how I could protect and nurture it. Who was I, really? What did I want to build in my life? These weren't questions I answered all at once, but the process of considering them became the foundation of who I am today.

The lesson I want to pass on to you is this: You are the architect of your identity. Each decision you make, each value you uphold, is a plank in the fence of your character. Take the time to understand what matters to you, your principles, your dreams, your sense of purpose. They will be the framework that guides you through life.

There are few things in life as important, or as elusive, as knowing who you truly are. In a world that often seems to tell us who to be, it's easy to lose sight of our own beliefs and values. But

I want you to understand this: no amount of external success or approval can replace the inner strength that comes from having a solid foundation of identity. This foundation, your true self, will give you a sense of purpose and direction, no matter where life takes you.

Identity isn't something that appears overnight. It's built, piece by piece, as you learn what resonates with you and what doesn't, what you stand for and what you can't abide by. To begin this journey, it's crucial to start by examining your values and beliefs. This is the core of who you are, the "why" behind every choice and action. When you know what truly matters to you, decisions become easier, relationships deepen, and your sense of self becomes more resilient.

Understanding Values: The Core of Who You Are

Values are the principles that guide our actions. They're the invisible compass that helps us navigate life. Some people value honesty above all else, while others prioritize kindness or ambition. Your values are deeply personal and may not look like anyone else's, but they're yours to embrace and live by.

To uncover your values, ask yourself questions like:

- What do I admire most in others?
- What qualities do I want to be known for?
- When do I feel most fulfilled and at peace?

Are there situations where I feel conflicted, and why?

Take time with these questions; they aren't meant to be answered quickly. Reflecting on moments in your life where you felt particularly proud, frustrated, or inspired can reveal a lot about your inner values. Maybe you felt an intense sense of pride when you stood up for someone or followed through on a commitment. Or perhaps you felt frustrated in a situation where integrity was compromised. These emotions are clues that can guide you toward identifying the values that matter most to you.

Once you identify your values, write them down. Keep them somewhere you can revisit, especially during difficult times. Life will challenge your values, there will be moments when the easy path would mean compromising them. But those moments are precisely when your values can act as a source of strength, helping you to stand firm and remain true to yourself.

Exploring Beliefs: The Mindsets that Shape You

Beliefs are closely tied to values, but they're slightly different. While values are more about principles, beliefs are the ideas we hold about ourselves, others, and the world. Beliefs can be empowering or limiting; they shape the way we interpret our experiences and influence how we approach challenges.

For example, believing in your ability to learn and grow makes it easier to tackle new challenges, while a belief that "I'm not good enough" can hold you back. Understanding your beliefs can be challenging, as some of them are so ingrained that we may not even realize they're there. They can come from childhood, family influences, cultural backgrounds, or past experiences.

To uncover your beliefs, reflect on these questions:

- How do I view myself? Do I believe I am capable and worthy?
- What do I believe about others? Do I trust people, or do I approach relationships with caution?
- What are my beliefs about success, failure, and happiness?

Sometimes, we hold beliefs that no longer serve us. Maybe you believe that vulnerability is a weakness, yet you long for deeper connections with others. Challenging these beliefs can be uncomfortable, but it's worth the discomfort. As you become aware of any limiting beliefs, ask yourself: Is this belief helping me or holding me back? Recognizing these limiting beliefs allows you to gradually replace them with more empowering ones.

Exercises to Identify What Matters Most

1. **The Mirror Test**

Stand in front of a mirror, look yourself in the eyes, and ask: "What do I want my life to stand for?" Let your response come from within, without overthinking. Sometimes, the simplest answers that emerge in these quiet moments are the truest. Repeat this exercise whenever you feel lost, and it may remind you of your core intentions.

2. **The Values Journal**

Set aside a notebook solely for exploring your values. Every day, write down moments when you felt a strong emotional response, positive or negative. Describe the situation and how it made you feel. Over time, look back at these entries to see if any patterns emerge. Do you notice that certain values, like honesty or compassion, consistently come up? This can help you pinpoint which values are most important to you.

3. **Visualizing Your Ideal Future**

Sit in a quiet place, close your eyes, and imagine yourself five, ten, even twenty years from now. Visualize your surroundings, the people in your life, the work you do, and how you feel. What principles are guiding your actions in this ideal future? What values are you embodying? This exercise helps you connect with the kind of person you want to become and can serve as a guide for your present-day choices.

4. **Defining Moments Reflection**

Think back on key moments that shaped you. These might be moments of triumph, failure, loss, or joy. What did these moments teach you about yourself and what matters most to you? Defining moments often highlight the values that resonate most deeply. Writing down these reflections can be a powerful way to clarify your beliefs and values.

Living by Your Values and Beliefs

Once you have a clearer sense of your values and beliefs, the next step is to actively integrate them into your daily life. This isn't always easy, and it won't happen overnight. Living authentically requires practice, patience, and a willingness to learn from your mistakes.

When you find yourself at a crossroads, use your values as a compass. Ask yourself, "Does this choice align with my core values?" If it doesn't, consider why you feel drawn to it. Sometimes, external pressures or fears can lead us toward choices that don't feel right. Trust your instincts, they're frequently a signal from your deeper self, guiding you toward the path that aligns with whom you truly are.

The Strength of Knowing Yourself

Building your identity is a lifelong journey, and there will be times when your values and beliefs evolve as you grow. Embrace this growth. Staying true to yourself doesn't mean you have to be rigid. As long as you're willing to honestly assess your actions and intentions, you'll remain grounded in who you are, even as you adapt to life's changes.

Remember, my son, knowing yourself is the greatest gift you can give not only to yourself but also to those around you. It allows you to live with integrity, to build meaningful connections, and to pursue a life that feels rich and fulfilling. When you know who you are, you become unshakable. You gain the strength to face challenges with courage, to stand tall in your values, and to find peace in the choices you make.

So take this time, whether it's a few moments each day, a quiet hour on a weekend, or a conversation with yourself in difficult times, to reflect on the foundation of your identity. As you build this foundation, know that you are creating something no one else can duplicate: the unique, valuable person you are meant to be.

Chapter 2: The Power of Authenticity

My son,

There was a time in my life when I almost let fear steal my authenticity. I was in my twenties, working my first real job in a fast-paced corporate environment. I was eager to prove myself, to climb the ladder, to be seen as someone capable and indispensable. And so, I wore a mask, not a physical one, but a figurative one made of compliance and conformity.

I remember a particular meeting with the senior management team. We were tasked with brainstorming solutions for a failing project. I had an idea, one that felt bold and a bit unconventional. But as I sat there, surrounded by confident voices and nodding heads, I hesitated. I could hear a voice in my head whispering, “What if they think it’s stupid? What if you embarrass yourself?” So, I stayed quiet.

Someone else eventually proposed a similar idea, and the room erupted in praise. The team embraced it, and the project turned around. I should have been relieved that the solution was found, but instead, I felt a pang of regret. Not because someone else got credit, but because I hadn’t trusted myself enough to speak up.

That moment stayed with me. It wasn’t about winning recognition; it was about the missed opportunity to be true to myself. I realized that I’d let fear of judgment silence me, and in doing so, I’d betrayed my own authenticity.

From that day forward, I made a promise to myself: I would always speak my truth, even if my voice shook. I wouldn’t suppress who I was to fit into someone else's mold. It wasn't easy at first, I stumbled and second-guessed myself, but every time I chose authenticity, I grew stronger. And something incredible happened: People began to trust me more, not because I had all the answers, but because I was honest and genuine.

Son, there will be times when staying true to yourself feels risky, when speaking up or showing your vulnerability feels terrifying. But I hope you'll remember this: The discomfort of authenticity is far better than the emptiness of living behind a mask. The world doesn't need more perfect impressions; it needs more people willing to be themselves, flaws and all.

In a World That Wants You to Conform

From the moment we're young, society surrounds us with expectations: how we should look, act, and think. These voices come from everywhere, family, friends, school, the media, and they can feel so loud that sometimes it's difficult to even hear your own. But at the end of the day, the most meaningful voice you have is the one within you. That's the voice of authenticity, your inner compass, guiding you to live in alignment with whom you truly are.

The journey to stay true to yourself in the face of pressure isn't easy, but it's one of the most important journeys you'll ever take. Being authentic means honoring what you value, what you believe, and who you are, even when it's hard, even when it makes you stand out, and even when you're tempted to blend in just to make things easier.

Why Authenticity Matters

When you live authentically, you're aligned with your core. This alignment brings a sense of peace and satisfaction that nothing else can. It helps you live without regrets, because you're not betraying yourself to meet others' expectations. Being authentic also allows you to form deeper, more meaningful connections. People who value you for who you are, rather than whom they want you to be; will stick by your side, and you'll feel a profound sense of belonging with them.

Inauthenticity, on the other hand, feels like constantly putting on a mask. Every time you bend to meet someone else's expectations or pretend to be someone you're not, a little piece of that mask chips away, reminding you of what you've sacrificed. Over time, this act of hiding wears you down. You might find success or acceptance, but it comes at a cost: you're never quite at ease, always feeling like something is missing, because you're not being true to yourself.

Recognizing Social Pressure

We all feel the weight of social pressure. It's human nature to want acceptance, and fitting in can feel comforting. But there's a difference between finding common ground with others and altering yourself to meet their approval.

Social pressure often comes in subtle forms: peer influence, cultural norms, or expectations from those we admire. You may feel the urge to change the way you act around different people, or to downplay parts of your personality to avoid judgment. And in today's digital age, social media amplifies this pressure by constantly showcasing idealized versions of life, making it easy to compare yourself to others.

Be mindful of these pressures, and remember that it's okay to challenge them. If you find yourself feeling the need to conform to please others, take a step back and ask yourself why. This awareness alone can help you recognize when you're being swayed and help you return to your authentic self.

Embracing Vulnerability

Authenticity requires vulnerability, and vulnerability can feel like weakness, but in reality, it's a strength. When you're authentic, you're willing to show up as you are, without hiding your flaws or fears. This openness takes courage because it means embracing the parts of yourself that you might worry others won't understand or accept.

Being vulnerable allows you to build trust with others and with yourself. When you're honest about your experiences and emotions, you invite others to do the same. This creates genuine connections that go beyond superficial friendships. Vulnerability reminds you that you're human, and it gives others permission to be human, too.

Resisting the Urge to Conform

One of the hardest parts of staying true to yourself is resisting the urge to conform. It's easy to slip into the habits or opinions of those around you, especially when doing so can make you feel like you belong. But true belonging comes from being accepted for who you are, not who you pretend to be.

Here's something I wish I'd known sooner: People who love you for your authenticity are the ones who will bring the most joy to your life. Yes, some people may disagree with you, and others may not understand your choices. But that's okay. Letting go of the need to be universally liked is liberating. When you focus on pleasing yourself rather than pleasing others, you'll find that the right people naturally gravitate toward you.

Finding Strength in Your Values

Your values serve as a foundation for authenticity. When you know what you believe and stand for, it becomes easier to resist social pressure. You don't have to adjust your behavior or opinions based on others' expectations; instead, you can draw strength from within.

Whenever you're tempted to compromise your values, remind yourself why they matter. Reflect on what they bring to your life and the sense of purpose they provide. Staying true to your values, even when it's difficult, builds resilience. And the more you practice aligning your actions with your beliefs, the stronger your sense of identity becomes.

The Joy of Self-Discovery

Living authentically means continuously discovering who you are. As you grow, you'll learn more about your strengths, passions, and quirks. This process of self-discovery is a lifelong journey, and it's one of the most rewarding experiences you'll ever have. Every time you make a choice that reflects your true self, you're not only deepening your understanding of who you are, but also strengthening your commitment to authenticity.

Give yourself the freedom to explore different aspects of your personality and interests. Don't be afraid to change your mind, to pursue new hobbies, or to walk a path that others may not understand. The more you embrace your uniqueness, the richer your life will be.

Exercises for Building Authenticity

Here are some practical exercises to help you cultivate and maintain authenticity:

1. Daily Reflection

Set aside time each evening to reflect on your day. Ask yourself, Did I live today in alignment with my true self? If you find moments where you felt inauthentic, think about why that happened. Understanding the reasons behind your actions can help you make choices that reflect your values more accurately in the future.

2. Embrace "I Don't Know"

It's natural to want to appear knowledgeable or certain, especially when others look to you for answers. But admitting that you don't know something is a powerful act of authenticity. Practice saying "I don't know" when you're unsure. It's a simple but effective way to build trust in yourself and others, allowing you to learn without the pressure of pretending to have all the answers.

3. Stand Up for Your Beliefs

Identify a belief that's important to you and look for opportunities to express it, even if it's in small ways. Maybe it's standing up for someone, being honest about your opinion, or sharing a personal story that reveals who you are. By practicing authenticity in small moments, you'll build the confidence to be true to yourself in larger, more challenging situations.

4. Create a Personal Manifesto

Write a brief manifesto that outlines your core values, beliefs, and goals. Keep it somewhere you can see it daily. This manifesto will serve as a reminder of who you are and the kind of life you want to lead. Revisiting it regularly can ground you and help you resist social pressure.

Staying True to Yourself

Living authentically is a practice. Some days, it will feel easy, while on others, it might take every ounce of strength you have. But every time you choose to stay true to yourself, you're building a life that reflects who you truly are—a life that brings fulfillment and peace. Authenticity isn't about achieving a perfect state; it's about continuously choosing to honor your values, beliefs, and identity.

As you go forward, remember that your authenticity is a gift not just to yourself, but to everyone around you. When you live openly and honestly, you encourage others to do the same. And in a world full of noise and expectations, your willingness to be yourself is an act of quiet, powerful bravery. Embrace this journey, my son, and know that no matter where life takes you, you'll always find a sense of home within your true self.

Chapter 3: Emotions and Resilience

Dear Son,

Emotions are powerful currents that move through each of us, sometimes gentle like a breeze, other times like a storm. They can be overwhelming, confusing, exhilarating, or even painful, and as you go through life, you'll experience a wide range of them. But there's a skill that can transform the way you navigate these emotional ups and downs: resilience.

Resilience doesn't mean suppressing or ignoring your feelings. Instead, it's about learning to manage them, to adapt, and to grow stronger from every experience. Emotions will ebb and flow, but when you cultivate resilience, you build an inner strength that helps you weather any storm.

The Power of Reflection

Let me share a moment that tested my own resilience.

Years ago, I was working on a project that demanded everything I had, time, effort, and emotional energy. I had poured countless late nights and weekends into it, believing that success was just within reach. When the big day came to present our results, I was brimming with hope, only to have my ideas dismissed outright in the meeting.

I remember walking out of that room, my heart heavy with disappointment. My first instinct was to dwell on the perceived failure, to question whether I was good enough, whether I even belonged in that role. For days, I carried the weight of that rejection like a storm cloud over my head.

But then, I decided to take a step back and reflect. What had gone wrong? Were there lessons hidden in the experience? As I replayed the situation in my mind, I began to see the gaps in my approach and the ways I could improve. Slowly, the sting of rejection transformed into a drive to grow.

That experience didn't just teach me to be better at my work; it taught me to be better at facing my emotions. I learned that resilience isn't about avoiding failure or rejection, but about finding the strength to learn from it and move forward.

Understanding Emotions

Emotions are messages. They reveal our needs, fears, hopes, and values. When you're feeling joy, it's often because something meaningful has happened; when you're angry, it's likely because you feel wronged or undervalued. When you're sad, there may be a loss or disappointment. Emotions are neither good nor bad, they're signals from within, helping us understand ourselves better.

Understanding your emotions begins with acknowledging them. In moments of intense feeling, ask yourself what's beneath the surface. Is it fear? Frustration? Hope? This awareness is the first step toward managing your emotions rather than letting them control you.

Embracing Vulnerability

Resilience frequently requires the courage to be vulnerable. Sometimes, this might mean sharing how you truly feel, even when it's uncomfortable. It can be tempting to hide emotions like sadness or fear, but allowing yourself to experience and express them is part of building resilience. Vulnerability reminds us that we're human, and sharing our emotions can strengthen relationships with others who genuinely care about us.

When you're open about your emotions, you're not only honoring your true self but also inviting others to support you. Vulnerability isn't a weakness; it's an essential aspect of resilience. By allowing yourself to feel, you're giving yourself the tools to heal and move forward.

Tools for Managing Emotions

Life will throw challenges your way, and there will be times when emotions seem to take over. Here are some tools to help you manage these emotional waves.

1. Mindfulness and Breathwork

One of the simplest and most effective ways to manage emotions is through mindfulness and breathwork. When emotions feel intense, take a moment to breathe deeply and slowly. Focus on each breath as it comes in and goes out. This helps ground you in the present moment, slowing down racing thoughts and calming your body.

2. Naming the Emotion

It might sound simple, but naming the emotion you're feeling can actually reduce its intensity. When you say, I'm feeling anxious, or "I'm feeling frustrated", you're taking a step back, observing the feeling rather than letting it consume you. Labeling the emotion allows you to examine it with a bit of distance, which can make it easier to address and work through.

3. Reframing Thoughts

Sometimes, our emotions are fueled by thoughts that aren't entirely accurate. For example, if you're feeling discouraged, it might be because you're thinking, "I'm not good enough" or "I'll never succeed." But are these thoughts truly grounded in reality, or are they just passing doubts?

Reframing is the process of challenging these negative thoughts and replacing them with more balanced perspectives. Instead of "I'll never succeed", try thinking, "I've faced challenges before, and I'm capable of handling this too."

4. Writing It Out

When emotions feel overwhelming, writing them down can be incredibly cathartic. Pouring your thoughts onto paper allows you to process your feelings, understand them better, and release some of the emotional weight. Writing gives you a safe space to be completely honest with yourself, without fear of judgment.

In moments of frustration or sadness, try writing a letter to yourself or to the situation causing these feelings. You don't have to share it with anyone; this exercise is for you. It helps to clarify your emotions and can often lead to insights you hadn't considered before.

5. Seeking Support

Resilience doesn't mean handling everything on your own. Asking for help or seeking advice is a sign of strength, not weakness. Whether it's friends, family, or a counselor, sharing your feelings with someone can provide comfort, new perspectives, and valuable guidance. Sometimes, just knowing that someone else understands can lighten your emotional load.

Building Resilience Through Self-Compassion

One of the most powerful components of resilience is self-compassion. In difficult moments, it's easy to criticize ourselves for not being stronger, faster, or better. But resilience isn't about perfection; it's about perseverance. Self-compassion means being gentle with yourself, especially in times of hardship.

When you stumble or make a mistake, remind yourself that it's okay. Everyone makes mistakes. Instead of focusing on what you did wrong, focus on what you can learn and how you can grow.

Strengthening Emotional Flexibility

Emotional resilience isn't about never feeling pain or disappointment. It's about being able to adapt, to bend rather than break when challenges arise. Life's unpredictability is certain, and being able to adjust to its highs and lows is part of emotional flexibility.

For example, when a plan falls apart or something doesn't go as expected, take a moment to accept it. Resilience doesn't mean forcing a positive outlook immediately, it means acknowledging reality, then choosing how to respond.

Finding Meaning in Adversity

Challenges can feel like setbacks, but they also offer opportunities for growth. Resilience is often strengthened through adversity. When life throws you a curveball, try to look for meaning within the struggle.

Finding meaning doesn't mean ignoring the pain—it means recognizing that even the hardest experiences can teach us something valuable.

Embracing Emotional Resilience

Son, resilience isn't a fixed trait; it's a skill you develop over time. There will be days when you feel incredibly strong, and days when you need to lean on others. Both are part of the journey. The important thing is to keep going, to continue building your emotional toolkit, and to treat yourself with patience and kindness along the way.

You'll face many challenges in life, and each one will shape you. With resilience, you're not just surviving these challenges; you're growing stronger because of them.

Embrace the journey, honor your emotions, and know that every step you take toward resilience is a step toward a more fulfilling, authentic life.

Part 2: Relationships with Others

As we navigate through life, the relationships we form with others become some of our greatest sources of joy, learning, and, at times, challenge. Family, friends, mentors, and partners all shape us in ways we often don't recognize until much later. The bonds we cultivate have the power to enrich our lives deeply, yet they require care, respect, and a willingness to understand perspectives beyond our own.

In this part, I want to share with you some guiding principles on building and maintaining meaningful connections. It's easy to take relationships for granted or assume that others will always understand us, but the truth is that relationships are an active, ongoing effort. Learning to communicate openly, forgive freely, and support others without losing sight of your own values will make you someone others trust and appreciate.

Ultimately, relationships aren't just about finding people who will be there for you; they're also about becoming someone who can be there for others. As you grow, I hope these insights help you nurture relationships that bring warmth, resilience, and wisdom into your life.

Chapter 4: The Power of Listening and Empathy

Son, if there's one skill that will shape the quality of your relationships and the depth of your connections, it's the art of listening. Listening is more than just hearing words; it's about understanding the person behind those words, sensing what's unspoken, and showing you truly care. This chapter is about the incredible power of listening and empathy, and how mastering them can build stronger, more fulfilling relationships.

Let me start by saying that real listening requires patience. It's not just about waiting for your turn to speak, but being genuinely interested in what someone else has to say. It means giving them your full attention, not because you're obligated, but because you want to understand their perspective. In a world that often moves too fast, being truly present for someone is a gift. When you give someone your undivided attention, you're telling them, "I see you. I value you."

When I was about your age, my father shared a moment with me that taught me the value of silence and truly listening. He had taken me to meet an old friend of his who was going through a difficult time after losing his job. For almost an hour, his friend poured out his worries and frustrations, while my father quietly listened, nodding now and then. Not once did he interrupt or try to offer a solution.

As we were leaving, I asked him why he hadn't given any advice or tried to comfort his friend with words. He simply smiled and said, "Sometimes, people don't need advice. They just require someone to listen. To feel like their voice matters." That moment has stayed with me, shaping the way I interact with others. Listening isn't about solving, it's about connecting.

Active Listening: Being Fully Present

Active listening is a skill, and like all skills, it requires practice. To truly listen actively, you have to focus on the speaker without letting your mind wander or planning what you're going to say next. Sometimes, silence is your greatest ally. Let there be pauses. Let the speaker finish their thoughts. If they pause, give them a moment to gather their thoughts. Typically, people reveal their true feelings in these quiet spaces between words.

Here are a few ways you can practice active listening:

1. Maintain Eye Contact

When someone is speaking to you, look them in the eyes. This doesn't mean staring, but it means showing that you're engaged and present. Eye contact is a powerful way to show respect and to let the other person know they have your attention.

2. Listen Without Interrupting

It's tempting to jump in, especially if you think you know what the person is going to say. But when you let someone speak without interruption, you're giving them the space to fully express themselves. Sometimes, in our eagerness to respond, we miss the most important parts of what they're trying to share.

3. Reflect Back

After the person has finished speaking, repeat back what you heard in your own words. This isn't just about parroting what they said; it's about showing that you've processed and understood. Try phrases like, "So what I'm hearing is…" or "It sounds like you're feeling…" This helps clarify any misunderstandings and shows the person you're really paying attention.

Understanding Empathy: Walking in Another's Shoes

Empathy goes hand in hand with listening. When you're empathetic, you're not just hearing words; you're connecting with the emotions behind them. You're putting yourself in someone else's shoes and trying to see the world through their eyes. Empathy is a bridge—it allows us to connect deeply with others, even when we don't fully understand their experiences.

Empathy doesn't mean you have to agree with everything someone says. Instead, it's about acknowledging their feelings, showing that you respect their experience, and being willing to see things from their perspective. This is how true understanding is built.

One way to cultivate empathy is by paying attention to non-verbal cues. Body language, facial expressions, tone of voice, all of these give clues about how someone is feeling. Pay attention to these signs. Notice if someone seems nervous, upset, or happy, even if their words don't directly say it. Empathy is about tuning into those unspoken signals.

Exercises to Build Empathy

Just like any other skill, empathy grows with practice. Here are some exercises that can help you develop a deeper sense of empathy in your everyday interactions:

1. Listen Without Judgment

The next time someone shares their perspective, listen without immediately forming opinions or judgments. Simply try to understand where they're coming from, even if you don't agree with them. Challenge yourself to ask questions that deepen your understanding rather than defend your own point of view.

2. Practice Perspective-Taking

Whenever you find yourself in a disagreement or feeling distant from someone, take a moment to put yourself in their shoes. Imagine what they might be feeling, thinking, or experiencing. Ask yourself, “If I were them, how would I feel?” This exercise can help you see situations from a new angle and approach conflicts with greater compassion.

3. Express Empathy in Conversations

When someone is talking to you about their challenges or difficulties, try responding with empathy rather than advice. For instance, if a friend says they’re having a tough day, instead of suggesting ways to fix it, you might say, “I’m sorry to hear that; it sounds really difficult. I’m here for you.” Sometimes, people don’t need solutions, they just need someone to listen and understand.

The Impact of Listening and Empathy on Relationships

As you go through life, you’ll realize that people remember not so much what you said, but how you made them feel. When you listen with an open heart and empathize with others, you create a safe space for genuine connection. People are drawn to those who make them feel understood and valued. Empathy is the foundation of trust, and trust is the cornerstone of any meaningful relationship.

Being an empathetic listener also helps in situations of conflict. When you approach a disagreement with empathy, you’re less likely to see the other person as an adversary. Instead, you’ll view them as someone with their own thoughts, feelings, and experiences. This shift in perspective makes it easier to resolve conflicts and find common ground.

Remember, empathy doesn't mean you always have to agree or sacrifice your own needs. It simply means being willing to understand another's perspective, even if it's different from your own. This is how you show respect for their humanity and foster a sense of connection.

Son, remember my story of my father's quiet strength at that moment of listening. He didn't need to say much to make a profound impact on his friend. It wasn't the advice he gave, or didn't give; that mattered. It was the presence, the understanding, and the empathy.

I hope you carry this lesson forward in your own life. Listening with an open heart and empathizing with others will not only strengthen your relationships but also enrich your own character. In a world that often feels rushed and disconnected, those who master these skills stand out as beacons of compassion and connection.

Chapter 5: Love and Friendship

Son, if there is one thing I want you to understand about love and friendship, it's this: not every connection will stand the test of time. Some people will come into your life like a gentle breeze, here for a moment and then gone. Others, however, will stay, becoming cornerstones of your life and supporting you through its highs and lows. The art lies in knowing which bonds to hold close, nurture, and understanding which ones are meant to drift away.

I'll share a story from my younger days. Back when I was starting out in my first job, I met someone I thought would be a lifelong friend. Let's call him David. David and I hit it off immediately—our shared sense of humor and ambition made the long workdays enjoyable. We spent countless hours talking about our dreams, sharing laughs, and supporting each other through the challenges of our early careers.

But as time passed, our paths began to diverge. David's priorities shifted, as did mine. Calls became sporadic, meetings rare, and eventually, we lost touch. At first, it felt like a failure—a relationship that hadn't withstood the test of time. But looking back, I realized David's presence during that phase of my life was exactly what I needed then. He taught me the importance of camaraderie and support, even if some bonds aren't meant to last forever.

On the other hand, there's your Uncle Michael. He and I met around the same time as David, but our friendship grew in a different way; steadily, withstanding the inevitable changes that life brought. Michael and I don't always agree, and we've had our share of disagreements, but the foundation of trust, shared values, and mutual respect has kept us close. Through all of life's ups and downs, he's been there.

This contrast taught me the difference between fleeting and lasting bonds. Not every connection is meant to endure, but every meaningful relationship, whether it lasts a season or a lifetime, brings its own lessons.

It's natural to meet many people over the course of your life. Some will bring excitement and novelty, while others will offer the comfort of stability. Fleeting connections are regularly those relationships that form quickly and might feel intense but are usually based on shared situations or interests that may change over time. These bonds can teach you valuable lessons, but they may not endure once the circumstances change.

Lasting relationships, on the other hand, grow gradually and are built on mutual respect, shared values, and a deep understanding of each other's character. These relationships may not always be flashy or exhilarating, but they offer a sense of security and authenticity that is hard to find elsewhere. Lasting bonds withstand time, distance, and even disagreements because they are rooted in something deeper than fleeting interests.

Here's a simple way to tell the difference: fleeting connections often revolve around convenience or circumstance, while meaningful bonds are based on a choice to stay connected, even when it's not easy.

Tips for Building Lasting Relationships

1. Be Genuine

Authenticity is the foundation of any meaningful relationship. Don't try to be someone you're not just to impress others. True friends and loved ones will accept you as you are, flaws and all. When you show your genuine self, you attract people who appreciate you for whom you truly are, not who you pretend to be.

2. Invest Time and Effort

Relationships don't thrive on autopilot. Just like any other meaningful endeavor, they require effort, patience, and time. Make it a point to reach out regularly, show up for important moments, and lend a listening ear. The more you invest in a relationship, the deeper and more meaningful it becomes.

3. Communicate Openly and Honestly

Open communication is key. Don't be afraid to express your feelings, concerns, and needs with those you care about. In a lasting relationship, honesty strengthens the bond, while secrets and dishonesty can slowly chip away at trust. Good communication builds mutual understanding, making it easier to work through any disagreements or misunderstandings that arise.

4. Be There in Both Good and Bad Times

A true friend or loved one is there not only to celebrate your victories but also to support you through challenges. If someone is only around when things are good, their loyalty may be superficial. Those who stay through the tough times are the ones you can count on, and that is the essence of a lasting relationship.

5. Celebrate the Differences

No two people are exactly alike, and that's a good thing. Differences in opinions, hobbies, or backgrounds can bring diversity to your life and offer new perspectives. Accepting these differences rather than trying to change each other strengthens the bond. After all, it's these unique traits that make each relationship special.

6. Practice Forgiveness and Patience

No one is perfect, and misunderstandings are bound to happen. Instead of holding grudges, practice forgiveness. Holding on to resentment only damages the relationship, while letting go can strengthen it. Relationships that last are built on forgiveness, patience, and the understanding that everyone makes mistakes.

Nurturing Love and Deepening Friendship

Love and friendship, like gardens, require care and attention to flourish. Here are some ways to nurture these connections, helping them grow stronger over time:

1. Show Appreciation

Take the time to let the people you care about know how much they mean to you. A simple "thank you" or a small gesture of kindness can go a long way in making someone feel valued. When people feel appreciated, they are more likely to invest in the relationship as well.

2. Be Present

In today's world, distractions are everywhere. Make an effort to be fully present when you're with loved ones. Put away your phone, listen attentively, and be engaged at the moment. Quality time is more valuable than quantity; even a short conversation can mean a lot if you're fully there.

3. Celebrate Each Other's Successes

True friends and loved ones don't feel envious of each other's accomplishments. Instead, they celebrate them wholeheartedly. When you cheer for someone's success, you reinforce the strength of your bond. Be the person who supports and uplifts, and you'll find that this energy often comes back to you in meaningful ways.

4. Respect Boundaries

Just because someone is close to you doesn't mean they won't have personal boundaries. Respect their need for space or time alone. Every relationship requires a healthy balance of togetherness and individuality. By respecting boundaries, you create a relationship built on trust and mutual respect.

5. Encourage Growth

Encourage your loved ones to pursue their passions, set new goals, and grow as individuals. A meaningful relationship isn't about keeping someone the same; it's about supporting them as they evolve. This support can deepen your bond, as both of you are constantly discovering new layers to each other.

6. Spend Quality Time Together

Shared experiences create memories and strengthen bonds. Make time to do things together, whether it's going for a walk, sharing a meal, or simply having a heartfelt conversation. It's often these simple moments that build the foundation of lasting relationships.

Recognizing and Letting Go of Fleeting Connections

Not all relationships are meant to last, and that's okay. Part of maturing is recognizing when a connection no longer serves you or when it's time to let go. If a relationship feels one-sided, lacks respect, or drains your energy, it may be time to step back. Remember, you have a limited amount of time and energy, and it's wise to invest it in relationships that are reciprocal and uplifting.

Ending a connection doesn't have to be a negative experience. Sometimes, people grow apart naturally. It doesn't mean the relationship wasn't valuable or meaningful at some point; it simply means it's time to move on. Trust that the right people will stay, and that those who leave have fulfilled their purpose in your life.

Cherishing the Bonds That Endure

Son, at the end of the day, the relationships that matter are the ones that make you feel supported, understood, and appreciated. They're the people you can rely on, the ones who stand by you no matter what, and who make your journey through life richer and more meaningful. Cherish these bonds. Don't take them for granted, and remember that meaningful relationships are among life's most precious gifts.

As you grow, you'll learn that love and friendship are about giving as much as receiving. Be the kind of friend and partner you want to have in your own life. Show loyalty, respect, and compassion, and you'll find that those who truly care about you will do the same. True relationships may be few, but they are a source of strength, joy, and resilience.

Remember, son, life's journey is far richer when shared with people who uplift, inspire, and love you. Nurture these bonds, for they are the foundation of a fulfilled and meaningful life.

Chapter 6: Handling Conflicts with Grace

Son, life isn't always smooth. No matter how well you get along with people or how deeply you care for them, there will come a time when you find yourself in a disagreement. Disagreements, when handled with maturity, can strengthen relationships rather than harm them. They teach us about ourselves and others, and they help us grow. The key lies in handling these moments with grace, calm, and respect.

When conflicts arise, it's natural to feel defensive or emotional. But approaching disagreements with a cool head allows you to make decisions you won't regret later. Let me share an example from my own life.

A Lesson from the Workshop

Years ago, I worked in a small workshop where tempers often flared. On one particular day, a disagreement with a colleague over a seemingly minor detail escalated into a heated argument. Neither of us was willing to back down, and the tension in the room was palpable.

I vividly remember storming out, convinced that I was in the right. But as I cooled off, I realized that the issue wasn't as black-and-white as it had seemed. The following day, instead of continuing the standoff, I approached my colleague with a simple question: "Can we talk?" We sat down, shared our perspectives calmly, and eventually discovered that the disagreement stemmed from a misunderstanding.

That conversation not only resolved our conflict but also strengthened our professional relationship. From that moment on, we collaborated with a newfound mutual respect, knowing that we could work through differences constructively.

This experience taught me that conflicts, when approached thoughtfully, can be opportunities to build trust and understanding.

Understanding the Nature of Conflict

The first step to handling conflict gracefully is to understand why conflicts happen. People come from different backgrounds, have different experiences, and see the world through different lenses. When two perspectives clashes, it's easy for misunderstandings to occur. But remember, a disagreement isn't necessarily a sign of failure or division. In fact, conflicts are natural and often necessary for growth. They encourage us to see things from another's point of view and, ultimately, to deepen our understanding of the people around us.

Conflicts can frequently feel personal, but they don't always have to be. Sometimes, they're simply the result of differing values, preferences, or beliefs. By understanding this, you can start to see disagreements as a natural part of human interaction rather than a threat.

Approaching Disagreements with Calm and Respect

When you're in the middle of a disagreement, it can feel tempting to raise your voice or dig in your heels. But son, remember that nothing good comes from reacting out of anger or frustration. It may feel difficult, but learning to approach conflicts with calm and respect is a powerful skill that will benefit you for a lifetime. Here's how:

1. Take a Breath Before Responding

When a conversation starts to get heated, pause and take a deep breath. This simple act can prevent you from saying something in the heat of the moment that you might later regret. By breathing deeply and calming yourself, you give yourself a moment to think clearly.

2. Listen First, Speak Second

Often, we're so eager to defend our point of view that we forget to really listen to the other person. But listening is one of the most powerful tools in conflict resolution. By letting the other person fully express

themselves, you may gain insights you hadn't considered before. Listening doesn't mean you agree with them; it just means you respect their perspective enough to hear it.

3. Use "I" Statements

When it's your turn to speak, avoid accusatory language. Instead of saying, "You always do this" or "You never listen," try using "I" statements. For example, "I feel unheard when this happens" or "I would appreciate it if we could work on this together." This small change in language can prevent the other person from feeling attacked and keeps the focus on finding a solution.

4. Keep the Goal in Mind

In the heat of a disagreement, it's easy to get sidetracked and focus on winning the argument. But remember, the goal isn't to win—it's to resolve the conflict and preserve the relationship. By keeping this goal in mind, you can approach the discussion with a collaborative mindset, which leads to more productive conversations.

Techniques for Constructive Conflict Resolution

Now that we've covered the mindset needed to approach conflicts, let's look at some specific techniques that can help you resolve disagreements constructively. These methods will not only help you navigate difficult conversations but also build stronger, more resilient relationships.

1. Find Common Ground

Even in the most heated conflicts, there's usually something you can agree on. Start the conversation by acknowledging any common ground. It could be as simple as agreeing on the importance of the relationship or recognizing that both of you care about the outcome. Finding common ground helps set a positive tone and reminds both parties that you're on the same team.

2. Focus on the Issue, Not the Person

When emotions run high, it's easy to turn disagreements into personal attacks. Avoid this by keeping the focus on the issue rather than the person. Instead of saying, "You're always late," try addressing the behavior: "When meetings start late, it affects the entire team's schedule." This approach allows for a more objective discussion and reduces defensiveness.

3. Seek to Understand Rather Than to Persuade

In conflicts, we often try to convince the other person of our point of view. But true resolution requires understanding, not persuasion. Try to put yourself in the other person's shoes. What are their concerns? What values are they trying to protect? When both parties feel understood, it's easier to find a middle ground.

4. Use Time-Outs When Needed

Sometimes, discussions can become too intense to continue productively. In these cases, it's okay to take a time-out. A break gives everyone time to cool off, gather their thoughts, and return to the conversation with a clearer mind. Just be sure to agree on a specific time to revisit the issue so it doesn't get ignored.

5. Offer Solutions, Not Just Criticisms

If there's a problem, try to approach it with a solution-focused mindset. Instead of dwelling on what went wrong, think about what can be done to improve things. Offering constructive solutions shows the other person that you're committed to making things better and prevents the conversation from becoming overly negative.

6. Agree to Disagree When Necessary

Not every conflict has to end with complete agreement. Sometimes, the most respectful resolution is to agree to disagree. Recognize that both perspectives have value, even if they differ. By accepting this, you can preserve the relationship without forcing a compromise that might not feel authentic.

The Long-Term Benefits of Graceful Conflict Resolution

Son, learning to handle conflicts with grace isn't just about solving immediate issues. It's about building a foundation of trust, respect, and understanding in your relationships. People who know that you can handle disagreements calmly and respectfully will feel safer and more open with you. They'll know that you won't judge them or abandon them over a difference of opinion.

This skill will serve you well in every area of life, from friendships and family relationships to professional settings. People who can navigate conflict gracefully are often seen as leaders and are trusted to handle challenging situations.

Practicing Forgiveness and Moving Forward

One of the hardest parts of resolving conflicts is letting go of any lingering resentment afterward. But holding onto grudges only hurts you. Forgiveness doesn't mean that you forget or condone what happened, it simply means that you're choosing not to let it weigh you down. By forgiving, you free yourself from the emotional burden of past disagreements and allow relationships to move forward.

To practice forgiveness, start by acknowledging your feelings. It's okay to feel hurt or disappointed. But don't let those feelings control your actions. Focus on the positive aspects of the relationship and remember that everyone makes mistakes, including you. Forgiveness is a gift that you give to yourself as much as to others.

Cultivating Inner Peace in Conflict Situations

Finally, remember that not all conflicts are external. Sometimes, the hardest conflicts are the ones we have with ourselves. We may feel torn between two choices, struggle with self-doubt, or feel conflicted about our own beliefs. Learning to handle these inner conflicts with grace is just as important as resolving conflicts with others.

When you find yourself in a battle with your own mind, treat yourself with the same respect and understanding that you would offer to someone else. Take time to listen to your feelings, seek to understand where they're coming from, and approach yourself with kindness. By cultivating inner peace, you equip yourself with a foundation of calm and confidence that helps in all areas of life.

Final Thoughts

Son, disagreements don't have to be destructive. In fact, when handled with grace, they can bring people closer together and deepen mutual respect. The ability to handle conflicts constructively will serve you well, not only in building strong relationships but also in developing resilience and empathy. Remember, a disagreement isn't about winning or losing; it's about growing and finding common ground.

By approaching conflicts with a mindset of respect, patience, and understanding, you'll be able to navigate even the toughest situations with confidence. Keep these principles close to your heart, and let them guide you whenever you face conflict, whether it's with others or within yourself.

Part 3: Work and Ambition

Son, as you step into adulthood, you'll find yourself facing new challenges and opportunities in the world of work. Ambition and the pursuit of a fulfilling career are central to building a life of purpose and independence. But it's easy to get swept up in the chase, running so fast toward success that you lose sight of what truly matters to you. In this part of our journey together, I want to share some thoughts on balancing ambition with integrity, finding work that fulfills rather than exhausts you, and building a career that reflects the values you hold dear.

Work is more than just a means to earn a living; it's an expression of who you are and what you stand for. It's the place where your talents meet the world's needs, where you contribute, grow, and learn. But ambition is a tricky companion; it can drive you to great heights, but if left unchecked, it can lead you astray. I want to help you harness that ambition in a way that strengthens, rather than weakens, your sense of self.

Throughout this section, we'll explore what it means to find a path that resonates with your values, cultivate the discipline and perseverance needed to thrive, and ultimately create a legacy that makes you proud. Remember, your work should never come at the expense of your wellbeing, nor should ambition cloud your kindness or humanity. Aim high, but stay grounded. Reach far, but stay true to yourself. This balance will be the foundation of a career, and a life worth building.

Chapter 7: Finding Your Path

Son, there's a moment in every young person's life where the question arises: What do I want to do with my life? Finding an answer can feel like searching for something elusive, but discovering your path is less about finding one "right" answer and more about choosing a direction that aligns with who you are at your core. Your path should reflect your values, interests, and unique strengths. Let me walk you through how you can start uncovering what truly calls to you.

I remember a time in my own life when I faced this very question. After finishing my studies, I stood at a crossroads, uncertain about which direction to take. I had an offer for a stable but uninspiring job, and I also had a dream to work in a field that fueled my creativity. At that moment, practicality seemed to outweigh passion, and I almost convinced myself to take the easier route. But then, I had a conversation with an old mentor, who asked me, "What's the one thing you could do every day, even if no one paid you for it?" That question stayed with me, and I realized that deep down, I wanted to create, to build, and to inspire.

The choice wasn't easy, but I took the road that aligned with my heart. It wasn't smooth sailing; it rarely is, but every challenge along the way felt meaningful because I was on a path that resonated with who I was. Son, I share this with you because I want you to know that finding your path requires courage, introspection, and a willingness to trust yourself.

Discovering Your Passions

When I talk about "passions," I don't mean you need to know exactly what you're destined to do. Rather, look for the things that energize you, the activities or ideas that make you feel alive. Pay attention to the moments when time seems to fly by or when you feel particularly engaged in what you're doing.

Exercise 1: Passion Exploration

Take some time this week to note down moments when you feel particularly engaged or fulfilled. Write down:

1. What you were doing
2. Who you were with
3. How it made you feel

Review this list and look for any patterns. You may find that you feel energized when working with your hands, interacting with people, solving complex problems, or helping others. These clues are valuable, they're the beginnings of understanding what brings you joy.

Choosing a Path Aligned with Your Values

As you identify what excites you, it's essential to also understand your values. Values are the principles that guide you, the beliefs you hold about what's most important in life. Aligning your career with your values will help you find a sense of purpose beyond mere achievement or financial success.

Exercise 2: Value Discovery

List out a few core values that resonate with you. Here are a few examples to consider:

- **Integrity**: Being honest and acting according to your moral principles.

- **Compassion**: Showing empathy and care for others.
- **Creativity**: Engaging in original thought or artistic expression.
- **Service**: Contributing to the welfare of others.

Write down five values that feel central to who you are. Think about the times in your life when you felt a strong sense of purpose or fulfillment, and identify the values that were present in those moments. Once you have a list, consider how these values might shape the kind of career you want.

For example, if "creativity" is a core value, then a role in a field that encourages innovation and self-expression may be fulfilling for you.

Matching Interests with Career Possibilities

One of the greatest challenges of choosing a path is seeing how your interests and values can fit into the working world. This is where some practical exploration can come into play. Consider fields that might allow you to use your passions and reflect your values.

Exercise 3: Career Exploration

Create a "career possibilities" list. Start with your values and interests, and research careers that align with them. Look into fields that spark your curiosity. Once you've listed some possibilities, research a bit deeper:

- Find out what daily life is like in that field.
- Look into educational or skill requirements.
- Identify entry points or ways to get hands-on experience.

Remember, you don't need to choose a single "dream job." Think of career paths as dynamic and flexible; you can always evolve in a role, and many people shift careers as they grow. What's important is that you're in a role that aligns with who you are at this point in your life.

Setting Your Compass: Goals and Intentions

Once you've explored potential paths, start setting a few initial goals. They don't have to be grand or set in stone, these are simply milestones to give you direction. Maybe you'd like to explore a specific career by taking an internship, or maybe you want to focus on developing a particular skill. Goals help you stay focused, but remember to stay flexible and open to change.

Exercise 4: Goal Setting

Choose three short-term goals that can help you explore your chosen path further. For example:

- Shadow a professional: Find someone in a field of interest and see if you can shadow them for a day.
- Develop a relevant skill: If your chosen path requires a specific skill, like public speaking, writing, or data analysis, begin working on it.
- Network and gather insights: Reach out to people in the industry and ask about their experiences, what they enjoy, and what challenges they face.

These steps don't lock you into a career, but they do allow you to gain insight into potential directions. Setting small, achievable goals will build your confidence as you learn more about where you might fit best.

Adapting Along the Way

Your path is yours to create, and sometimes, the destination changes. As you grow, you may find new interests or realize that certain aspects of your work no longer fulfill you. It's okay to pivot, to adjust, and to find new ways to align your work with your values.

As you move forward, listen to yourself and stay curious. Keep asking questions about what you want out of life, and remember that it's okay if the answers change. Each experience adds a piece to the mosaic of your life, shaping you into the person you are meant to become.

Your path, son, will be uniquely yours. Trust yourself, keep an open mind, and remember that I'm here to support you every step of the way. Finding a meaningful career isn't about having all the answers, it's about starting with a clear intention, being willing to explore, and staying true to what you hold dear. That's the foundation for a fulfilling, purposeful life.

Chapter 8: Work Ethic and Perseverance

Son, there's a strength that comes not from talent or luck, but from the will to keep going, to put in effort even when things get tough, and to stay steady even when the finish line seems far away. That's what we call work ethic and perseverance. These qualities might not be flashy, but they are powerful. They're what make the difference between people who simply start and those who eventually succeed.

Let me share a story from my own life that taught me the true value of perseverance. When I was your age, I worked a summer job building fences. It wasn't glamorous work, and the days were long under the sun. One morning, my supervisor assigned me to dig post holes in particularly rocky ground. After hours of exhausting effort with little progress, I considered asking to be reassigned to an easier task. But something stopped me. I thought about how quitting would feel versus how finishing, despite the struggle, might feel.

So, I decided to keep going. I focused on one post hole at a time, breaking the work into smaller, manageable parts. By the end of the day, I had completed the task, and though I was sore and tired, I felt a pride I hadn't expected. The satisfaction of pushing through something difficult taught me that effort, no matter how small, builds character and resilience.

Son, I want you to know that you don't have to tackle every challenge all at once. Perseverance isn't about being unbreakable, it's about being willing to try, again and again, even when it's hard.

The Value of Effort

Talent alone is rarely enough. The most successful people are often not the ones who started with the most advantages, but those who put in the most effort. Putting in effort means committing yourself fully to whatever you choose to do, understanding that progress often comes in small, steady steps.

Effort shows up in different ways: staying focused, not cutting corners, and showing up each day ready to give your best. It may feel easier to take shortcuts, but the satisfaction that comes from knowing you've done your best cannot be bought or faked. Whatever field you enter, be the one who is willing to go the extra mile. Work hard not only for the results but also for the pride of knowing you gave your all.

Exercise 1: Building a Habit of Effort

Start small. Select a task each day, something manageable but meaningful, and give it your full attention and energy. Maybe it's your studies, maybe it's a sport or a personal project. Commit to giving that task your best effort each day. Over time, you'll notice that this practice strengthens your work ethic, building a foundation of commitment that will carry over into larger areas of your life.

Discipline: The Backbone of Success

Discipline is the silent force behind great achievements. It's not about harshness or rigidity, but about consistency and a steady focus on your goals, day in and day out. With discipline, you can make progress even on the days you don't feel motivated or energized.

The Power of Small, Consistent Actions

It's easy to imagine that big achievements happen in moments of brilliance, but often they're the result of steady, repeated actions. Waking up early to exercise, putting in time to study or practice, taking care of your responsibilities, these small actions, done consistently, add up over time.

Think of discipline as a muscle that needs regular exercise. The more you use it, the stronger it becomes. Set daily routines and stick to them, even when you don't feel like it. Over time, discipline will become a habit, something that carries you forward even when you feel tired or discouraged.

Exercise 2: Building Discipline through Routine

Set a small goal that you can practice daily for one month. It could be waking up at a certain time, reading a chapter of a book each day, or dedicating a fixed amount of time to a skill you want to develop. Write down your progress and reflect on how you feel as you follow through each day. This practice will help you build a foundation of discipline that can support larger goals.

Embracing Obstacles as Learning Opportunities

Challenges and setbacks are inevitable, but they are also opportunities for growth. Each time you encounter a problem, you have the chance to learn something new, to adapt, and to become stronger. Perseverance is not about avoiding difficulties, but about facing them with a mindset that says, "I will find a way through this."

Think about a tree with deep roots. It can withstand strong winds because its roots hold firm. Perseverance is like those roots; it grounds you, allowing you to stand firm even when challenges arise. When you embrace obstacles as part of your journey, they become stepping stones rather than roadblocks.

Strategy 1: Reframe Your Challenges

The next time you face a difficult situation, try to reframe it as a learning experience. Instead of asking, "Why is this happening to me?" ask, "What can I learn from this?" This shift in perspective can turn frustration into resilience, helping you grow stronger with each challenge you face.

Staying Motivated Through Setbacks

Motivation can come and go, but when you're committed to your goals, you'll find ways to keep moving even on tough days. When you feel like giving up, remember the reasons why you started. Sometimes, stepping back to reconnect with your purpose can reignite your motivation and help you push through.

Also, remember that progress is often not visible in the short term. Growth happens gradually, and sometimes it's only when we look back that we see how far we've come. Don't let setbacks discourage you. They are often a sign that you're pushing your limits and growing.

Strategy 2: The Power of Visualizing Your Goals

When you're feeling discouraged, take a moment to close your eyes and visualize the outcome you're working toward. Imagine yourself achieving your goals and experiencing the pride, joy, and satisfaction that comes with it. This exercise can be a powerful reminder of what you're working toward and why the journey is worth it.

Overcoming Fear of Failure

Fear of failure is a common barrier to perseverance. Many people avoid trying new things or give up easily because they fear making mistakes. But remember, failure is a teacher. Every mistake holds a lesson, and each attempt you make, even if unsuccessful, brings you closer to success.

As long as you keep trying, you haven't truly failed. Each setback gives you new information, allowing you to approach the challenge with more knowledge and insight the next time.

Strategy 3: Embrace a Growth Mindset

View every failure as part of your learning process. Understand that mastery takes time, and each attempt, whether successful or not, is a step forward. Write down what you learn from each setback, and use these lessons as tools to strengthen your resilience.

Putting It All Together

Son, work ethic and perseverance aren't just about hard work, they're about resilience, patience, and the willingness to keep moving forward even when the path gets rocky. There will be days when the effort feels heavy, and motivation seems distant. But in those moments, remember that your journey is built on the choices you make each day, the strength you cultivate in overcoming challenges, and the determination you bring to your goals.

I can't promise that every day will be easy, but I can tell you that the rewards of perseverance are real. The satisfaction of knowing you've done your best, of seeing your efforts pay off, and of achieving what once seemed out of reach, these are the gifts of hard work and resilience.

Keep these lessons close to your heart, and never underestimate the power of steady, consistent effort. Your path won't always be smooth, but with a strong work ethic and the courage to persevere, you will find your way forward.

Chapter 9: Thriving in What You Do

Finding fulfillment in work is one of the most rewarding yet challenging pursuits. When work aligns with your passions and values, it becomes more than just a means to earn a living; it becomes a source of purpose and pride. However, sustaining motivation, balancing personal and professional life, and avoiding burnout are vital elements that make this journey truly fulfilling. Thriving in what you do is about more than chasing achievements, it's about cultivating joy, motivation, and a sense of balance, all of which help you bring your best self into your work and beyond.

Staying Motivated and Finding Fulfillment

One of the greatest drivers of motivation is a sense of purpose. Purpose keeps you going through the difficult days, the setbacks, and the obstacles. When you have a clear "why" behind what you do, every task takes on meaning. However, purpose isn't static; it evolves over time, and so must your understanding of what drives you.

An Anecdote from My Own Journey

Let me share a story from my early career. I had just started a new job, eager to prove myself, but the challenges were more than I anticipated. There were long nights, demanding deadlines, and moments of doubt. One evening, after weeks of relentless effort, I considered quitting. It felt like I was pouring everything into a well with no bottom.

That night, I remembered a conversation I'd had with my father. He told me about his first business venture, selling handmade goods in the local market. The business struggled initially, but instead of giving up, he focused on improving his craft and building relationships with customers. Slowly but surely, his persistence paid off, and the little market stall became a trusted name in the community.

His story gave me a new perspective. I realized that success rarely comes quickly, it's built on steady effort and a clear sense of purpose. With that lesson in mind, I redoubled my efforts. Weeks turned into months, and the challenges didn't disappear, but my perspective shifted. I began to see growth in myself and results in my work.

The Importance of Setting Personal Goals

Motivation often dips when you lose sight of your goals. Setting clear, meaningful goals gives you something tangible to work toward, both in the short and long term. Identify goals that excite you, challenge you, and push you out of your comfort zone. These could be related to acquiring new skills, achieving a promotion, or even improving work-life balance. When you have clear goals, you feel a sense of accomplishment each time you take a step closer, and this propels you forward.

Aligning Work with Personal Values

Fulfillment comes when you feel that your work aligns with your personal values. If you value creativity, seek opportunities that allow you to express it. If you value helping others, find ways to incorporate this into your job. The closer your work aligns with your values, the easier it is to feel a sense of purpose and satisfaction in what you do.

Celebrating Small Wins

Progress is often incremental, so celebrating small achievements along the way helps keep motivation high. Each milestone you reach, no matter how small, deserves acknowledgment. These small victories add up over time and remind you of the progress you're making. Celebrating these wins with gratitude builds confidence, satisfaction, and a positive association with the work you're doing.

Balancing Personal and Professional Life

A fulfilling life isn't solely built on career achievements; it's a harmonious blend of professional success and personal happiness. Striking a balance

between the two is essential to thrive in both areas, and to avoid the burnout that can drain your energy and enthusiasm for work.

Setting Boundaries to Maintain Balance

Boundaries are essential in maintaining a healthy balance between work and personal life. It's easy to become so wrapped up in work that personal time takes a backseat. However, setting clear boundaries, such as designated "no-work" hours or not answering emails after a certain time, protects your personal time and ensures you have space to recharge.

Prioritizing Self-Care

Self-care is crucial for maintaining motivation and preventing burnout. Engaging in activities outside of work that bring you joy, relaxation, or a sense of accomplishment can refresh your mind and keep you motivated in your professional life. Exercise, hobbies, time spent with family or friends, or even quiet time alone can provide balance and recharge your energy.

Building a Support System

Having a support system, both at work and outside, can make a tremendous difference in how you manage your personal and professional life. Friends, family, and colleagues who understand and support your goals help you stay grounded. At work, mentors or trusted colleagues can offer guidance, encouragement, and sometimes a fresh perspective, making it easier to handle challenges while keeping personal life in focus.

Tips for Maintaining Motivation Over Time

Even with purpose and balance, there will be days when motivation wanes. Staying consistently motivated requires intentional practices to keep you engaged and enthusiastic about your work.

Embracing a Growth Mindset

A growth mindset; believing that your abilities can develop over time, can significantly impact your motivation. Viewing challenges as opportunities to learn rather than setbacks keeps you focused on growth. When you encounter difficulties, remind yourself that they are temporary hurdles and that each one offers a chance to strengthen your skills and resilience.

Continuing to Learn and Improve

Learning keeps you engaged and prevents stagnation. When you actively seek opportunities to expand your knowledge or skills, work becomes more interesting and fulfilling. This might mean taking on new projects, attending workshops, or even reading about your field. As you learn and improve, you'll feel more competent, confident, and motivated to pursue your goals.

Reflecting on Accomplishments

Regularly take time to reflect on what you've achieved. Looking back at your accomplishments, both big and small, can help you recognize the impact of your efforts. Reflecting on your progress reinforces your sense of purpose, reminding you why you started this journey in the first place. This reflection can reignite motivation and refocus your energy on what truly matters.

Avoiding Burnout: Recognizing When to Rest

Burnout is a risk for anyone deeply invested in their work. Over time, stress, exhaustion, and a lack of balance can lead to burnout, which not only affects your productivity but can also drain your joy and motivation.

Recognizing the Signs of Burnout

Burnout can creep up slowly, often showing up as irritability, fatigue, and a lack of enthusiasm for work. You may find yourself feeling disconnected, overly stressed, or exhausted even after a full night's sleep. Recognizing these signs early allows you to take steps to address them before burnout fully sets in.

Taking Time to Recharge

To thrive in your work, you must regularly recharge. Time away from work is not a luxury; it's a necessity. Take breaks throughout the day, go for a walk, or spend time with loved ones. Taking weekends or vacations to unplug and relax gives your mind and body the rest they need, allowing you to return to work refreshed and ready to engage fully.

Practicing Mindfulness and Gratitude

Mindfulness, being fully present in each moment, can help reduce stress and increase resilience. It helps you stay centered, keeping your mind from wandering to past regrets or future worries. Gratitude, on the other hand, shifts your focus to what you have rather than what you lack. Together, mindfulness and gratitude bring a sense of peace and perspective, which can reignite motivation and prevent burnout.

Ultimately, success in your career isn't just about external achievements; it's about finding joy, balance, and purpose in what you do. It's about building a life where your work complements and enhances your personal happiness rather than overshadowing it. When you are intentional about your goals, mindful of your balance, and resilient in the face of challenges, you'll find that motivation and fulfillment become natural companions on your journey.

By investing in your work ethic, balancing your personal and professional life, and nurturing motivation, you create a path where you don't just survive; you thrive. And as you continue to grow and succeed, remember that thriving is a dynamic process; it's about being adaptable, learning from each experience, and continuously building a life that reflects your best self.

Part 4: The Art of Living

Life is often described as an art, a tapestry woven from countless choices, moments, and experiences that create the story of who we are and how we live. In this part, we delve into the nuances of living fully, gracefully, and with a heart that remains open to the world. The art of living isn't about perfection; it's about resilience, wisdom, and the pursuit of meaning.

At its core, living well means embracing each day with purpose, balancing the challenges and joys, and finding contentment in both the ordinary and extraordinary. It means becoming a student of life itself, learning from our experiences and the people we encounter, and letting our values guide us. Each of us has our own journey, yet within each day lies the universal challenge of finding meaning, connection, and peace.

As you move forward, consider what it means to create a life that truly reflects who you are. These chapters explore timeless principles to cultivate a life rich in gratitude, resilience, and joy. Life, after all, is more than a list of accomplishments; it's a mosaic of choices and connections that define us. Embracing the art of living means seeking growth and peace in equal measure, learning when to push forward and when to let go, and above all, treasuring each moment.

Chapter 10: Gratitude and Simplicity

In a world filled with constant noise and endless pursuits, it's easy to overlook the beauty of the small, quiet moments that fill our days. Gratitude and simplicity are two guiding principles that remind us to pause, notice, and appreciate the richness of life as it is. Living with gratitude transforms the ordinary into the extraordinary, helping us see beyond daily stress and inviting us to find joy in the simplest things. Embracing simplicity, in turn, allows us to focus on what truly matters, shedding the excess and reconnecting with what makes us feel grounded and alive.

The ability to appreciate life's small joys and cultivate a habit of gratitude opens us up to a more fulfilling, contented life. Rather than racing through each day, it's about slowing down enough to notice the details, the fleeting smiles, the warm sunlight, and the connections that surround us. This chapter explores the transformative effects of gratitude and simplicity, along with practical exercises to help you nurture these qualities in your own life. When you learn to appreciate what you have and let go of what you don't need, you create space for peace, happiness, and true abundance.

The Power of Gratitude: Shifting Focus to What Matters

Gratitude isn't merely a reaction to receiving something good; it's a mindset, a deliberate choice to notice and appreciate what we have, no matter how small or ordinary. When you embrace gratitude, you shift your focus from what you lack to what you already possess, creating a profound sense of abundance.

Growing up, my father often shared a simple yet powerful memory from his childhood. He grew up in a small village, where life was humble, and resources were scarce. Every evening, his family would gather outside their modest home to watch the sun set over the hills, sipping tea brewed from wild herbs. "The tea wasn't remarkable, and the chairs creaked under us," he would say, "but those moments were gold."

What made those evenings special wasn't the tea or the view, but the connection they shared and the gratitude they felt for each other's presence. They didn't need wealth to feel wealthy, they only needed to notice and appreciate the small joys that life offered. His story taught me a timeless lesson: gratitude transforms the ordinary into the extraordinary.

Why Gratitude Matters

Research has shown that gratitude has immense psychological and physical benefits. People who regularly practice gratitude tend to be happier, healthier, and more resilient. Gratitude reduces stress, enhances positive emotions, and builds stronger relationships. By focusing on the positives, you train your brain to look for the good in situations, which can transform your outlook on life and the way you interact with the world.

Gratitude also fosters empathy and compassion, allowing you to better understand and connect with others. When you recognize the kindness or generosity of others, it's natural to want to return it, creating a ripple effect that spreads kindness and positivity. Practicing gratitude doesn't mean ignoring life's challenges; rather, it gives you a way to cope with difficulties by focusing on what remains steady and good.

Cultivating a Gratitude Practice

Building a habit of gratitude takes time and intentionality. Here are some ways to incorporate gratitude into your daily routine:

1. Daily Gratitude Journaling: Spend a few minutes each day writing down three things you're grateful for. These don't need to be grand or life-changing; they can be as simple as a warm cup of tea or a friendly conversation. Over time, this habit trains your mind to notice the positive aspects of each day.

2. Reflective Moments: Set aside moments throughout the day to pause and reflect. Whether it's during your morning coffee or right before bed, take a few minutes to reflect on the blessings in your life. Regularly bringing gratitude into your routine helps embed it in your daily thinking.

3. Expressing Thanks to Others: Acknowledging others is a powerful way to cultivate gratitude. Write a thank-you note or express appreciation to someone who's had a positive impact on your life. Not only does this strengthen your connection with others, but it also reinforces the habit of recognizing and valuing kindness.

4. Mindful Gratitude: Practice mindfulness by fully immersing yourself in moments that bring joy or peace. For example, if you're watching a sunset, take a moment to really notice its colors and feel gratitude for its beauty. This mindfulness helps deepen your appreciation for the small joys.

Embracing Simplicity: Making Space for What Matters

Simplicity is more than just decluttering physical possessions; it's a philosophy that encourages you to clear away distractions and focus on what brings you true happiness. In a culture that often equates more with better, simplicity allows you to break free from the pressures to accumulate, consume, and constantly strive for more. Instead, it invites you to embrace a life centered on purpose, clarity, and peace.

My father's tea ritual was also a testament to the beauty of simplicity. Their family didn't have expensive furniture, exotic foods, or grand entertainment. Yet, those unassuming evenings became some of the most cherished moments of his life. "We didn't have much, but we always had enough," he'd say with a smile.

That sense of "enough" came from valuing what truly mattered: love, togetherness, and the ability to savor a moment. Simplicity helps us recognize that we don't need more to feel fulfilled; we only need to focus on the essentials and shed what doesn't serve us.

The Benefits of Simplifying

When you simplify, you reduce mental and emotional clutter, creating space for inner calm and clarity. Simplicity allows you to live more intentionally, making it easier to focus on your values, passions, and relationships. By letting go of excess, you free yourself from the weight of things that don't add meaning to your life, giving you room to cultivate deeper connections, joy, and a sense of purpose.

Practical Steps to Embrace Simplicity

1. Declutter Your Space: Start by clearing out items that no longer serve a purpose. When you create a physical environment that is free of excess, you'll find that it often has a calming effect on your mind as well. Choose items that genuinely add value or happiness to your life, and let go of the rest.

2. Limit Digital Distractions: Our digital lives can quickly become overwhelming. Try setting boundaries around technology use, such as designating "no-screen" times or limiting social media. Reducing digital distractions frees up time for meaningful activities, such as reading, spending time with loved ones, or pursuing hobbies.

3. Prioritize Quality over Quantity: Simplicity isn't about deprivation; it's about selecting quality over quantity. This might mean buying fewer, but better-made items, or spending time with a few close friends rather than a large group. Focusing on quality helps you find greater satisfaction in what you have.

4. Practice Saying No: Part of simplicity is learning to protect your time and energy. Saying no to activities or obligations that don't align with your values frees you to invest in what truly matters. Honoring your time helps you maintain a sense of peace and prevents burnout.

Exercises for Gratitude and Simplicity

The following exercises can help you further develop a gratitude mindset and embrace a simpler, more intentional way of living.

1. Gratitude Reflection Exercise: Take a moment each evening to reflect on three things you're grateful for, as well as why they're meaningful to you. This could include people, experiences, or even qualities about yourself. Write them down in a journal, taking a few minutes to feel genuine appreciation for each.

2. Simple Living Audit: Reflect on areas in your life where you can simplify. This could be your home, schedule, or digital use. Choose one area to start with and make a plan to reduce or reorganize it to better align with your values. This practice not only declutters your environment but also helps clarify what's most important to you.

3. Gratitude Visualization: Spend a few minutes visualizing something or someone you're grateful for, and immerse yourself in the feeling of appreciation. Imagine the positive emotions you feel around this person or experience, and allow gratitude to expand in your heart.

4. Prioritize Your Week: At the beginning of each week, list your priorities based on what truly matters. Are there tasks or commitments that you could let go of? Is there room to add something that brings joy or meaning? This practice helps you align your time with your values.

Choosing a Life of Contentment

The beauty of gratitude and simplicity is that they shift your focus from what's missing to what's already here. A life centered on gratitude brings you closer to contentment and peace, allowing you to find joy in even the most ordinary moments. Simplicity helps you see the value in enough, to let go of the constant striving for more, and to appreciate the life you're living right now.

Ultimately, the journey of gratitude and simplicity is about cultivating a life where you can find happiness in the everyday, a life where you're connected to what truly matters. It's about filling your days with meaningful connections, appreciating life's small pleasures, and realizing that sometimes, less really is more. Living with gratitude and simplicity reminds us that true wealth doesn't come from things; it comes from the richness of experiences, relationships, and the peace that comes with knowing you have enough.

Chapter 11: Time Management and Priorities

Son, there's one resource in life we can never replenish: time. It's our most valuable asset, slipping through our fingers every moment, and how we choose to spend it shapes who we are and the lives we build. I want you to understand that managing your time isn't just about fitting everything in; it's about dedicating yourself to what truly matters, finding balance, and creating a life of purpose.

Time management isn't just a skill, it's a philosophy. It's about selecting what you stand for, what you value, and aligning your actions to reflect that. When you know how to spend your time well, you'll find you have room for what truly matters, even as life gets busier and more complex. Today, I want to share with you the importance of balancing priorities, setting goals, and using your time wisely. It's about understanding that each moment is an opportunity, a chance to grow, connect, learn, and become who you're meant to be.

The Essence of Time: Understanding Its Value

When we're young, time feels limitless. Hours stretch out, summers seem endless, and waiting for anything feels like an eternity. But as you grow, you'll notice that time passes faster. Days and weeks blur together, and it can feel like there's never enough time to do everything. That's why I want you to realize early on that time is something you must invest wisely. Each moment you spend is gone forever, so the goal is to spend those moments in a way that fills you with purpose and satisfaction.

Take a moment and ask yourself: "What matters most to me? What do I want to look back on and feel proud of?" When you have clarity on these questions, managing your time becomes less about checking off tasks and more about living with intention.

Knowing Your Priorities

One of the biggest lessons I've learned is that not everything in life is equally important. There will always be more demands on your time than you can handle, and it's up to you to determine what truly deserves your attention. Knowing your priorities gives you a compass to navigate the decisions and challenges of life.

My father often shared a memory that has stayed with me. As a young man, he worked long hours to provide for his family, frequently juggling multiple responsibilities. But no matter how busy he was, he made it a point to set aside Sunday afternoons for us. We'd sit together, sharing a simple meal, talking about the week, or playing a game of chess. "These hours are sacred," he'd say. "Work will always be there, but these moments with you won't."

His actions taught me that while work and obligations are significant, they should never overshadow what truly matters. By carving out time for his family, he showed me the power of intentionality, of choosing to prioritize what's irreplaceable.

This memory reminds me to ask myself, "Am I spending my time on what truly matters?" It's a question that has guided me through life's busyness and helped me refocus when I've felt overwhelmed.

Exercise: Setting Your Priorities

To help you clarify your priorities, take a few minutes to write down the things that matter most to you. These might include relationships, health, learning, career ambitions, hobbies, or personal growth. Once you've listed them, rank them by importance.

This exercise will reveal what you value most and will help you focus on the areas that deserve your time and energy.

Having clear priorities doesn't mean you'll never make mistakes or lose focus, but it does give you a roadmap to return to when life feels overwhelming. When you know what matters most, you can say "no" to the distractions and obligations that don't serve you.

The Power of Goals

Once you're clear on your priorities, the next step is to set goals that align with them. Goals provide structure to your time. They transform your dreams into actionable steps and give you a reason to wake up each day with purpose. When setting goals, remember to make them specific and realistic.

Here's a technique that might help you: the SMART method. Make sure each goal is:

- **Specific**: Clearly define what you want to achieve.
- **Measurable**: Identify a way to track your progress.
- **Achievable**: Set a goal that is realistic within your abilities and resources.
- **Relevant**: Align the goal with your priorities and values.
- **Time-bound**: Set a timeframe to help you stay focused.

For example, if one of your top priorities is health, a SMART goal could be, "I will go for a 30-minute jog three times a week for the next month." This is specific, measurable, and achievable, and it has a clear timeline. By setting goals, you create stepping stones that guide you towards a fulfilling life, one step at a time.

Practical Tools for Managing Your Time

Time management isn't about cramming as much as possible into each day. Instead, it's about organizing your time to ensure you're dedicating yourself to what matters most. Here are some methods that I think you'll find helpful as you grow:

1. The Eisenhower Matrix

This is a simple but effective way to categorize tasks. Imagine dividing tasks into four categories:

- Urgent and Important: Tasks that need immediate attention (e.g., studying for tomorrow's test).
- Important but Not Urgent: Tasks that are significant but can be scheduled (e.g., starting a fitness routine).
- Urgent but Not Important: Tasks that are pressing but may not add much value (e.g., replying to a non-urgent message).
- Not Urgent and Not Important: Tasks that don't truly contribute to your goals (e.g., mindlessly browsing social media).

This method helps you identify what genuinely deserves your time. By focusing on the tasks in the first two categories, you can make progress on what matters without getting sidetracked by distractions.

2. Time Blocking

Time blocking involves dedicating specific blocks of time to different activities or tasks. For example, you could schedule time each morning for focused work, set aside afternoons for exercise or hobbies, and reserve evenings for relaxation or family time. By giving each part of your day a purpose, you avoid wasting time and keep yourself focused.

3. The Pomodoro Technique

This technique involves working in focused intervals (usually 25 minutes), followed by a short break. After four cycles, you take a longer break. This method encourages deep focus and can be particularly useful for tasks that require sustained concentration. It's a reminder to take regular breaks and prevent burnout, keeping your mind sharp and your motivation strong.

4. The Rule of Three

Every morning, write down three tasks that you want to complete by the end of the day. These should be tasks that align with your goals and priorities. Focusing on three key tasks helps prevent you from becoming overwhelmed by a long to-do list and ensures that each day moves you closer to your bigger ambitions.

Flexibility and Adaptability

While it's important to have a plan, life rarely goes exactly as we expect. There will be days when things don't go as planned, and that's okay. True time management involves learning to adapt without losing sight of your priorities. If something unexpected comes up, adjust your plan and return to your priorities as soon as possible. Flexibility is key because it keeps you moving forward even when things don't go perfectly.

The Balance of Work and Rest

Son, remember that rest is just as significant as work. Our society often glorifies busyness, but rest is essential to recharge and maintain motivation. Taking time for yourself is not a luxury; it's a necessity. Whether it's reading, spending time outdoors, or simply relaxing with family, make sure you're giving yourself space to breathe.

When I think about balance, I'm reminded again of my father's Sundays. While his weekdays were consumed by work, those afternoons of laughter and connection were his way of recharging. He understood that rest wasn't about idleness, it was about creating the energy to give his best in every other part of life.

That balance, that rhythm of work and rest, is something I've come to value deeply. It's not about achieving perfection, but about ensuring that you have time for both your ambitions and the moments that make life rich and meaningful.

Honoring Your Unique Rhythm

Each of us has a unique rhythm, a natural pattern for when we feel most alert, focused, or creative. Some people are early risers, while others find their best energy in the afternoon or evening. Pay attention to when you feel most productive and align your most important tasks with those times. Working with your natural energy flow, instead of against it, can make a significant difference in how much you accomplish.

Living with Purpose

At the heart of time management is the desire to live with purpose, to spend your moments on what truly counts. When you're clear on your values and priorities, each day becomes an opportunity to make choices that align with your vision of a meaningful life. You'll start to see your time as a tool for building the life you want, rather than something you're trying to "manage."

Son, the goal isn't to fit everything into each day or to be productive every second. The goal is to live with intention, to invest your time in ways that bring you joy, fulfillment, and growth. By balancing your time well, you create a life that is not only successful but deeply satisfying.

Chapter 12: Creating a Lasting Legacy

Son, when we talk about legacy, we're not just talking about what people will say about us once we're gone. It's deeper than that; it's about the ripple effect of our choices, values, and actions on the world. Legacy is the part of ourselves we leave behind, living on through the people we've touched, the ideas we've sparked, and the positive changes we've helped bring into existence. It's the testament of a life lived with intention and purpose, a life that wasn't just about accumulating, achieving, or even succeeding, but about giving something meaningful to the world.

An Anecdote: The Seed of Gratitude

When I was your age, I vividly remember a moment with my own father. One spring, he spent hours planting a small apple tree in the corner of our yard. It wasn't a grand gesture, just a simple act of care for the earth. I asked him why he was so meticulous, why he spent so much time nurturing something that would take years to bear fruit. He smiled and said, "This tree might never grow big enough for me to enjoy its shade, but one day, you or someone else will. That's the beauty of it; it's not about me; it's about what I leave for others."

Years later, when that tree stood tall and abundant with apples, I realized what he meant. His quiet act of planting wasn't just about the tree; it was about teaching me the importance of thinking beyond myself, of contributing to a future I might not fully see. That tree became a living symbol of his legacy, a reminder of his values, and a lesson I carry with me to this day.

Understanding Legacy: Beyond Material Wealth

Often, people think of legacy in terms of material wealth or family heirlooms passed down through generations. While these can certainly be part of it, a true legacy goes beyond wealth or possessions. It's about the values you instill, the love you share, and the wisdom you impart. It's about being a positive force in the lives of others, whether through kindness, support, or inspiration.

Imagine legacy as a garden you've tended throughout your life. The seeds you plant, your actions, values, and relationships, grow into something beautiful, providing shelter, nourishment, and inspiration for others, even after you're no longer around to tend it. Remember, son, a legacy is built in everyday moments, in small but meaningful ways, in the kindnesses you extend, and in the integrity you maintain.

Reflecting on What You Want to Leave Behind

Creating a legacy begins with introspection. Take some time to ask yourself these questions: What do I want to be remembered for? What values do I want to pass on? What impact do I want to have on the people around me and the world at large? When you reflect on these questions, you're not just imagining a distant future; you're shaping the principles that guide you today.

Exercise: Define Your Core Values

To build a meaningful legacy, start by clarifying the values that are most important to you. Take a sheet of paper, and write down the values that resonate with you, words like honesty, kindness, resilience, courage, or compassion. Once you've written them down, pick your top three. These are the values that you feel are essential to who you are and what you want to represent. They will be your guiding lights, influencing your choices, actions, and the impact you have on others.

When you're clear on your values, it becomes easier to make decisions and live in a way that aligns with the legacy you wish to leave. Each choice you make, big or small, becomes an opportunity to express these values, and in doing so, you begin to craft a legacy that reflects who you are at your core.

Living Your Legacy: Small Actions, Big Impact

Legacy isn't something you create at the end of your life; it's something you build every day. It's in the way you treat people, the respect you show, and the effort you put into being a force for good in the world. Often, we overlook the power of small actions, but remember that even a simple act of kindness can ripple outward, influencing others in ways we may never fully see.

For instance, helping a friend in need, encouraging someone who's struggling, or standing up for what's right even when it's hard, these are all ways of living your legacy. People remember not just what you did, but how you made them feel. By making a habit of positive actions, you start to leave a trail of impact, one that speaks to your values and touches others on a deeply personal level.

Exercise: Write a Legacy Statement

A legacy statement is a personal mission that captures the essence of the impact you want to have on the world. It doesn't have to be long or complicated. Here's an example to get you started: "I want to be remembered as someone who spread kindness, shared wisdom, and inspired others to be true to themselves." Take some time to craft a legacy statement that resonates with you. This statement can serve as a reminder of the kind of person you want to be and the kind of impact you want to make.

The Power of Influence: How You Shape Others

Son, as you go through life, you'll influence people in ways you may not even realize. Every interaction is a chance to uplift, encourage, and inspire. Whether it's a casual conversation or a deep friendship, your words, and actions have the power to shape others' lives. Legacy isn't always about grand gestures; sometimes, it's about being a role model in small, consistent ways.

Think about the people who have influenced you the most. What did they do that left such a lasting impression? Perhaps it was their patience, their wisdom, or their unwavering belief in you. In the same way, you can influence others by being present, listening deeply, and showing that you care. This is a legacy that transcends time, as the people you've influenced go on to influence others, creating a chain of positive impact that extends beyond your lifetime.

Leaving a Legacy of Kindness and Compassion

In a world that often seems to move at a relentless pace, kindness and compassion are gifts that can't be overestimated. When you treat others with respect and empathy, you're creating a legacy of humanity, showing that despite life's challenges, it's possible to remain caring and considerate. Kindness has a way of multiplying; one compassionate act can inspire another, setting off a chain reaction of goodwill.

Remember that true kindness isn't about expecting something in return; it's about giving without attachment, knowing that the joy of helping someone else is its own reward. By embodying kindness and compassion, you create a legacy that makes a genuine difference in people's lives.

Ways to Influence the World Positively

Creating a lasting legacy also involves making a positive impact on the broader world. Here are a few ways to start:

1. **Mentorship**: Share your knowledge and experiences with others, especially those who may benefit from your guidance. Mentorship allows you to pass on lessons you've learned, helping others grow and succeed.

2. **Volunteer Work**: Give your time and energy to causes that align with your values. Whether it's supporting your community, helping the environment, or standing up for social justice, volunteer work is a powerful way to create change.

3. **Creativity and Innovation**: Use your talents to create something meaningful. Whether through art, writing, or other forms of expression, your work can inspire and influence others, leaving a legacy of creativity.

4. **Environmental Stewardship**: Caring for the environment is one of the most impactful ways to leave a legacy. By being mindful of how you treat the planet, you contribute to a better future for generations to come.

5. **Advocacy**: Stand up for what you believe in, whether it's equality, education, or freedom. By advocating for positive change, you help create a world where people can thrive.

Building a Legacy of Integrity

Finally, remember that integrity is the foundation of a lasting legacy. Living with integrity means staying true to your values, even when it's difficult. People respect those who are genuine and honest, and they remember those who stood by their principles. When you live with integrity, you create a legacy that others can admire, trust, and look up to.

The Ripple Effect: A Legacy That Outlives You

One of the most beautiful things about legacy is its ability to ripple outward, affecting people you may never meet. When you live with intention, compassion, and purpose, your actions influence others in ways that carry on. Your friends, family, and even strangers you've helped may take a part of your spirit with them, passing it on to others in turn. This is the essence of a lasting legacy; one that outlives you and continues to touch lives for generations.

Embracing the Journey

Creating a legacy isn't a final destination; it's a lifelong journey. It's about committing to growth, to kindness, and to living a life that reflects your values. Along the way, you'll make mistakes, learn lessons, and evolve, but what matters most is that you remain true to the impact you want to leave behind. Each day, you have the chance to build your legacy, one choice, one action at a time.

Son, as you go forward in life, know that your legacy is a living testament to who you are. It's the culmination of your choices, the manifestation of your values, and the impact of your kindness. Live with the awareness that each moment is an opportunity to contribute to something greater than yourself, to leave a piece of yourself in the world that speaks to the person you've become.

Conclusion: A Final Word of Love and Pride

Son, as I bring these words to a close, I find myself filled with a quiet pride and an overwhelming sense of love. Writing to you like this has been more than just a transfer of knowledge; it's been a journey, a way to share the essence of what I hope for you, to offer the lessons that life has gifted me, sometimes with open hands, other times with clenched fists. If there's one thing I want you to know, beyond all the advice and all the wisdom, it's that you have everything you need inside of you to lead a meaningful life.

The world will offer its fair share of obstacles, but you have strength within you that can withstand any storm. You are capable, and you are resilient. In you, I see the possibility of not just a good life but a life that can inspire others, a life that is true to your values and driven by your passions.

Remember, you don't have to be perfect. Perfection is a mirage, something that distracts rather than defines us. What matters is that you show up in this world as the best version of yourself, grounded in honesty and compassion. You will make mistakes; we all do. But those moments, difficult as they may be, are a part of the journey. They are not there to break you, but to build you, to teach you more about yourself than success ever could.

As your father, I have my own dreams for you, but the greatest of them is for you to find joy, to find peace, and to live with purpose. I want you to wake up each day knowing that you are loved, knowing that who you are is more than enough. If I've learned anything in this life, it's that love, love for oneself, love for others, love for life, is the foundation on which all else stands. Without it, our accomplishments feel hollow, our achievements seem fleeting. But with love, every small moment, every simple joy becomes a treasure.

Let love guide you, let kindness be your compass. Know that the legacy you leave will be shaped not just by what you do, but by how you do it. The world doesn't always remember our words, but it remembers our actions, the warmth we brought, the smiles we shared, the lives we touched.

No matter where life takes you, know that I am endlessly proud of you. I am proud of your heart, your strength, your determination. I am proud of the man you are becoming. And I am grateful, grateful to have had the chance to share these thoughts with you, to offer a glimpse of what's possible for you in this vast, unpredictable world.

As you continue forward, keep these words close to you. They are just words, yes, but they are also a piece of me, a piece of my heart, my hopes, and my love for you. Carry them with you, but know that they are only here to support you on your journey, to remind you of what is possible. The rest is yours to create, to discover, to make your own.

And so, my son, may your life be filled with purpose, your days rich with joy, and your heart always grounded in love.

With all my love,

Your father

www.ingramcontent.com/pod-product-compliance
Lightning Source LLC
LaVergne TN
LVHW010458160826
845677LV00012B/2541

* 9 7 9 8 2 3 0 4 2 5 3 5 9 *